REAL COUNTRY

poems by

Michael Harty

Finishing Line Press
Georgetown, Kentucky

REAL COUNTRY

Copyright © 2023 by Michael Harty
ISBN 979-8-88838-294-3 First Edition
All rights reserved under International and Pan-American Copyright Conventions. No part of this book may be reproduced in any manner whatsoever without written permission from the publisher, except in the case of brief quotations embodied in critical articles and reviews.

ACKNOWLEDGMENTS

Thanks to the following publications, where some of these poems have appeared previously:

Texas Poetry Calendar: "Pillagers"
New Directions Journal: "You Were Nameless"
I-70 Review: "Blue Steel"
New Letters: "What Jesus Would Do"
"Poetry Monday", International Psychoanalysis website: "Jackknife in Your Jeans"
Coal City Review: "Country School"

Publisher: Leah Huete de Maines
Editor: Christen Kincaid
Cover Art: Kilian-Seiler, Unsplash.com
Author Photo: Jean Harty
Cover Design: Elizabeth Maines McCleavy

Order online: www.finishinglinepress.com
also available on amazon.com

Author inquiries and mail orders:
Finishing Line Press
PO Box 1626
Georgetown, Kentucky 40324
USA

Table of Contents

Pillagers 1

Accidental Hedgerow 2

Storm Shelter 3

You Were Nameless 4

Blue Steel 5

What Jesús Would Do 6

Discipline 7

Jackknife in Your Jeans 9

Dominoes 10

Warning 11

Hayride 12

Big Hill 13

Country School 14

Paralyzer 16

Schoolboy Stock Show 18

farm road incident 20

The English Teacher I Wish I Could Remember with Gratitude 21

In Our Part of Texas, Prohibition Ended in the Sixties 22

"This is KOMA, Broadcasting from Oklahoma City!" 24

The world of the farm kid is not well known any more, except by the diminishing number who still live in it. It is, or was, a world of big spaces and small schools, of long bus rides and short sentences. These poems come out of a West Texas version of that experience from a few decades ago. I hope they preserve something real and recognizable even in the midst of the increasingly homogenized, media-saturated culture of today,

Pillagers

We must have been dizzy, must have drunk
too deeply of all that space around us,
city boys moved to the country, away
from alleys and sidewalks and houses next door.

Must have tasted the same elixir
as conquering armies, resistance suddenly
vanished, restraint forgotten, opportunity everywhere.
We looked for things to ravage.

Found an outbuilding next to the water well,
laid siege with clods and rocks and BB guns.
Not a window survived. Doorway breached,
interior looted of its rusty machine parts,

floor crunching with glass shards
and we joyful amid the wreckage
that whole summer of transgression,
entranced by the music of smashing jars.

Accidental Hedgerow

An old fenceline had trapped
a tangle of tumbleweeds that in turn
captured the blowing sand. Seeds
of prairie grasses dropped
undigested from passing birds
could root and join the rusted wire
in the buried armature of a dune,
narrow, north and south, growing itself
year by year into the landscape.

It was a place for small
adventures just large enough for us.
To poke stick into burrow
ready to leap back
from the unknown beast.
Follow the odor of death
to the place a coyote had dragged
his stolen chickens. Once
to spy a green collared lizard,
a foot-long dragon
never seen before or since.

Only a few yards between fields
but even in dry times wide enough
to spread our imaginations.
And when rains flooded the ditches
we would wriggle in the brown
currents like naked salamanders
then walk the brief peninsula
in the rainwater lake
to study hieroglyphs
on the shells of box turtles,
serenaded by the shrill
pulsing of little frogs.

Storm Shelter

It was always there, halfway
between house and barn,
mounded up like the grave
of some forgotten monster,
a hump bare of grass because
it was all subsoil, excavated
clay and caliche. A hinged
trapdoor with a rope handle
we were not to touch unless
it was an emergency, which meant
either a tornado heading for the house
or Russian bombers overhead.

When an emergency happened
it was a hot afternoon in May,
clouds boiling and the daylight
tinted purple and green. We couldn't
hear sirens but we could watch
the slender funnel feeling for the ground,
pulling back, then returning full-grown
to seize and ravish whatever it could.
That time we grabbed an armload
of blankets and the transistor radio,
piled down the dark splintery steps,
latched the door and waited
among the shelves with their cobwebbed
supply of Vienna sausage and extra batteries.

We climbed out at twilight, the house
still standing, the clouds smooth again.
That was it. We never did have to hide
from the Russians, although at school
there were under-the-desk drills
twice a year. We told each other
the bombs, if they came, were bound
to miss us. When it came to taking shelter,
the truth is, we were more afraid of the spiders.

You Were Nameless

The things we taught ourselves
to believe: you children of hot-blooded people
would not need coats. At recess
you liked to field grounders
bare-handed. You didn't want to read with us.
You were slow. You were happy.

We knew to stay away
from your smell of woodsmoke and Catholicism.
Switchblades. Head lice.

A faded purple bus with green
fenders and Mexican plates
stood among the shacks. Perhaps
someone lived in the purple bus. I never knew.

Eyes shadowed down and away, you climbed
the three metal steps of our bus (official yellow)
as if they were a mountain.
Silent in your seat you might have seen
fathers and mothers, older brothers
early in the fields, bowed
over cotton rows, leaning into the straps
of nine-foot bags dragging behind.

From across the aisle
we watched anonymous birds
flock to earth, gabble in bird language,
then rise together in a cloud,
secret signals telling all at once,
the season is over, it is time to go.

Perdoname, por favor, no he entendido.
Please forgive me, I did not understand.

Blue Steel

My friend Benny taught me
to pump the air rifle
extra strokes to add power.
One of the outbuildings
had ventilation holes we used
as gunports. Visibility was best
in winter, when sparrows
couldn't hide in the leaves.

Ten years old, that's the time
to learn about taking life.
You grow more skillful,
your breath steadies,
whatever is in your sights
shrinks until it's in your power.

Dozens of murders. A blackbird died
in the middle of mating,
triumphant flutter collapsing,
a bright stain in the alfalfa.
The nighthawk that used to scribe
wild zigzags on the summer evening
flopped broken from its day-perch.

On the album Johnny Cash
sang of shooting a man
just to watch him die,
and the prisoners roared approval.
I heard it and didn't flinch.
I'd held the blue steel in my hand.

What Jesús Would Do

He would hoist my dusty canvas sack
to the hook below the spring scale, keeping
the shoulder strap clear of the ground.

He would mark the weight in a small notebook,
pocket the pencil stub, then help drag
the sack up and over, into the wire-sided
flimsy trailer, where I'd shake out
my seventy or eighty pounds of cotton.

He'd offer a drink from his canteen
before he pointed me to my next row.

He would speak careful English to me,
quick Spanish to members of his crew.

He would watch me pick alongside them, straddling
the row, thrusting spiky wads of fluff
back into the long bag until I imagined
I could be dragging a dead body. Sometimes

he would take a sack himself, finish off
two rows while the next man did one,
fan himself with his straw hat in the shade.

He would weigh my last load by flashlight,
total up my pay for the day's work, a dollar fifty
a hundred pounds. He didn't say a thing
about handing over those crumpled bills
to me and not his own brothers and nephews.

Anything I wondered, I never asked.
On Monday I was going back to school.

Discipline

Just an ordinary amount
of mischief up and down the aisle,
old Bus No. 4 on its morning rounds,
the driver, let's call him Coach,
squinting at the mirror,
two high school girls in the seat
behind him comparing boyfriends,
seventh-grade boys passing a Playboy
when his eyes are on the road.
Farther back I'm getting my daily sex
education from my friend Ronnie
whose older sister likes to try
out her fantasies on him.
Then a dumb sixth-grader Billy Ray
decides to impress a girl
in the second row by shooting her
from behind with a rubber band
which misses
and bounces off the windshield.

Not a word spoken. Coach
pulls the bus to the shoulder,
sets the emergency brake, rises
and comes down the aisle. Stands
over Billy Ray, almost gently
takes him by the arm.
Reaches under his seat on the way
out the door, pulls out
the paddle. Beside the road
in the first row of stubble
he turns Billy Ray toward the bus
so we can all watch his face,
bends him over with a hand
on the back of his neck,
swings the paddle well back
and swiftly forward hard enough
to lift the kid onto his toes. Twice.

Still not a word as we watch
Billy Ray climb the steps red-faced
and blinking, look away
from the girl in the second row,
find his seat. The bus moves on

and it's a school day
like any other. Except that afternoon
at recess stupid Billy Ray
gets in more trouble
for picking a fight, giving
some fourth-grader a bloody nose.

Jackknife in Your Jeans

You knew it was there
in the front pocket, right there
with the quarter for lunch, the nickel
for a Milky Way—you carried metal undetected,
unsuspected, free to come and go. You knew
the bone polish of its flanks,
honed burnish of its blade:
spit on the whetstone, rub circles
to perfect the edge. Remember
the tidy heft of it, how you gauged it
just right to make it turn
once and a half in the air, stick
between your buddy's feet. No fear
unless some greasy stranger
two years older, still in your grade,
flashed a danger-blade six inches long,
snick-click and you imagined
bloody slash, tight circle jab-dance,
hold on, this is way too serious. Stick
to the friendly corner of the schoolyard,
a practice place. Maybe the principal
came out in his shirt sleeves
to show you a trick. Across the way girls
might turn from their jacks and jump-ropes,
whisper something new and old, something
you needed to grasp, but that would come
later: time on your side,
room in your pocket,
the blade folded away.

Dominoes

One May when I was twelve
a whole year's precipitation came at once.
Young cotton and maize
survived the hail, but now
with no drainage, rainwater lakes everywhere,
the plants were drowning. It could be weeks
before a man could get into the fields,
and no way to know if he could replant
with a chance for a crop.

My uncle drove me in his pickup
to the cotton gin office
where the farmers gathered
for coffee and smokes. I heard laughter:
they were playing dominoes.
I said I didn't understand.
How could they play a game
at a time like this?
They could lose everything
and there they sat laughing.

He said a man's only got so much time
and so much worry in him.
He don't waste it on things he can't change.
Them fellows have fed their livestock,
their tractors are gassed up,
and they already done their prayin'.
You think they should hang around the house,
yell at the kids, make the wife miserable?
If you ain't gonna draw a bumper crop, maybe
you can still draw a double five. Let 'em play.

On the way home I asked him
would he teach me the game.

Warning

After dark from anywhere in the county
the red signal was in the sky,
twenty stories up, blinking planes away.

Country kids watched it from their cars,
parked between fields
to explore each other.

Once there was a sensation
when a girl disappeared. For six days
her name was a headline.

We learned the boyfriend did it,
strangled her then scraped out
a shallow grave in a grain field.

He told the sheriff he feared to lose
his commission at the air base
when she claimed she was pregnant.

The autopsy confirmed it. Some people
sympathized with him, getting
mixed up with the wrong kind of girl.

We lived far away, other side
of the county, but after that
if we found a shriveled condom

discarded along a turn-row
we would pause, take a breath,
search a few yards into the field.

Hayride

A kid named Tommy
affected by the moon
or the same hormones
as the rest of us
jumped off the trailer
tried to jump back on
missed his grip and the wheel
crushed his shoulder. Later
he said he was fortunate
it wasn't his neck
in a cast for six weeks.

The rest of us, not so lucky.
The driver turned back
to meet the ambulance
meaning that among the bales
many blankets were not shared
nor shy kisses exchanged
and many who had hoped
to return from the ride
a little less virginal
waited yet again to start learning
what chances we might take,
what injuries we might suffer,
how badly we would fall
and whether we would get up.

Big Hill

Teachers could use his first name but to us
he was Big Hill: six-four and shaggy, long-armed,

hard-muscled and farmer-tanned from hours
on the tractor, stubble-jawed and frowning

when one of us cowed freshmen crossed his path.
We were careful not to look him in the face.

Picture in the yearbook: he grabs a rebound
and shakes it, a wolf breaking a rabbit's neck.

Never a heavy word to me, but hallway air
breathed easier the next year, when he'd graduated.

Later, he didn't come back from the war. Someone
who knew him remembered that he'd always been kind.

Country School

Ramshackle hog pen,
far edge of the school grounds
where the fields began.
A dozen thirty-pound weaners
we'd feed all fall and winter,
market in spring to pay
for the Future Farmers banquet.

It was how we freshman
ag students (all the boys)
learned to drive stick shift,
every other week taking our turn
at the green Chevy pickup
that mostly stood rusting
in its space by the shop.
Two at a time excused
from Mr. Howell's afternoon drone
of dairy breeds, growing seasons,
fertilizer formulas. Buckle on
coveralls, slip into pigpen shoes,
crank up the Chevy,
don't grind the gears.

At the lunchroom's back door
galvanized barrels, the day's
swine-diet, red beans, wilted salad,
jello and hominy and half-eaten burgers
sloshed together, hoisted,
hauled and dumped.

The job got dangerous
in January, hogs two hundred pounds
and ice on the trough
but hurry and there was time
for a smoke behind the shed, stretch
the hour to the limit
then a quick stick

of Dentyne and return
the truck to its space,
coveralls to the hook
to hang ready for the next time
the keys were in your hand
and pig shit smelled like freedom.

Paralyzer

"Now boys, you got to understand about these old boars."
Raymond Howell, our Vo-Ag teacher.
"They hit four years old, six hundred,
seven hundred pounds, too big
to service anything but a great big sow.
Put him on one of them little gilts,
he'll just crush her. Plus, when he's been at it
that long, he's plumb wore out,
shootin' blanks, can't do his job. So
what do we do? Right, cull him out,
turn him into bacon. But here's the problem.
His meat's gonna be all musky, worthless
unless you castrate him first, give
that rankness time to get out of his system.
And that's what we're here for."

Somebody said, ain't it dangerous, him so big?
"Not if you're smart, you'll see, we'll get him
with the paralyzer, it'll be real quick."
What was a paralyzer? I pictured
some apparatus, bars and clamps
to keep him motionless. Or a big syringe,
lay him out with an injection
so he's unconscious when the deed is done.
But we came to the pen, the boar waiting,
red-eyed, humped, and massive,
and the paralyzer was just a loop of cable
passed into the boar's mouth, drawn tight
around the upper jaw, behind the stumps
of tusks, and anchored at the other end
to a fencepost set in concrete.

And it worked. Some gene must have dictated
that when the boar felt that forward pull,
he had only one answer. He roared
and squealed and foamed at the mouth
but strained in one direction only, backward. Meanwhile,
Howell took the pocketknife he'd whetted earlier,
stepped around behind the hog and directed
a student to hold the tail aside
while he made a quick vertical slash
through the corrugated skin of the scrotum.
He reached in to extract a softball-size
testicle trailing knotty veins and cords,
which he scraped with the knife
until they parted. "Don't want to cut 'em
too clean," he said, "this way they clot better."

Same operation on the other side, then he tossed
the removed organs into the next pen,
where the sows nosed and nibbled at them.
The bleeding incisions he sprayed with orange chemical
to prevent screw-worms, and he was done.
It had taken maybe three minutes in all.
The boar, now technically a stag, wobbled
to the water trough. In a couple of weeks
his wounds would heal, his flesh
would be edible, and he'd be shipped
to the slaughterhouse. But if he considered
such matters at all, he probably
believed he'd been fighting back.
When we turned him loose,
maybe he thought he'd won.

Schoolboy Stock Show

First Friday in April all eight school buses
were parked on the playground, their barn
taken over, an exhibition hall for the day.
Rows of six-by-six straw-filled pens,
aisles between that led to the show ring,
so narrow a lady in a straight skirt
once got a snout between the knees
and a ten-yard piggyback ride. In our boots
and wide-brimmed hats we labored
with shampoos and oils, clippers and combs, frantic
pampering against the hour for judging.
And perhaps on the sly for an extra edge,
gallons of water down the calf's throat
to increase its bulk, or a finger-full
of mentholatum under the pig's tail
to put a proper arch in its back.

And then to the ring, first the lambs
posing foursquare, poked and stroked
by the judge: how springy the wool?
How firm the layer of fat? Then the swine,
class by class, milling about the ring,
anxious owners steering them with canes,
breaking up fights, maneuvering to give the judge
a view of heavy hams, sleek sides, trim jowls.
And finally the calves, milk-fed
to a thousand pounds, chain-led
in a ponderous waddle to their places
in a line that would be shuffled
and re-ordered as the judge came
to his rankings. Ribbons awarded
on the spot, yellows and reds and blues,
and for the grand champions, purple rosettes
with twenty-dollar bills. No auction here,
bids rising into the thousands, winners
funding a year of college; it was trailer
the animals home, clear the straw, retrieve
the exiled buses, get ready for Monday.

But already as we cleaned our boots
and hung away the blue FFA jackets
we were looking to the time next winter
when we'd pack our overnight bags

with poker decks and rum-soaked cigarillos,
pile into one of those long yellow buses,
ag teacher at the wheel and carefully
unobservant father-chaperones in the front seats,
and head across the state to Fort Worth,
the biggest stock show of the year,
a city with hotels ten stories tall
and rummies on the streets who'd take
a dollar to score us a pint of vodka
and give us our taste of the big time.

farm road incident

so many warnings but
the one time
it happened no one
was speeding no one drinking
my friend drove
carefully in the fog some field hand
tractored onto the pavement
panic swerve the world
in slow motion
upside down no safety
belts in the pickup
coming to rest headlights
pointed back the way
we came I saw the empty
seat beside me was he underneath
and the relief when I found
him unhurt staggering
in the roadway that was when
I started to tremble

**The English Teacher I Wish I Could
Remember with Gratitude**

I won't use her name, it makes me ashamed.
She was young, no more than 25.

When she stood in front of the class
she never smiled. We mocked her behind her back,

also because she was heavy, also
because she sometimes stammered.

Also because she walked with a limp. In later years
I heard it was from a rodeo injury.

Rodeo? She never told us that story about herself.
Of course, we never gave her the chance.

No matter how she tried, we sat
silent as rocks in her class, played dumb,

even those of us who loved to read,
even those who could tell she was not the enemy.

I don't remember a single word she taught.
When I remember her, she's in tears.

In Our Part of Texas, Prohibition Ended in the Sixties

Pinky's had a grand opening
in time for the weekend
and U.S. 84 changed overnight
from sleepy two-lane to crowded raceway
along a thirty-mile stretch north
from the precinct down in Garza County
that voted itself wet and immediately
became the only oasis in a hundred miles.

The word was out, and hot-rods, Cadillacs,
pickups and jalopies crowded in,
swooping down from that level
monochrome above the Caprock
where it was dry as buffalo bones,
joining the red crawl of tail lights
on a downhill mile that glowed
with pink neon at the end.

We were right there among them,
me in the back with Joe Mack alongside,
Tom-Tom driving his low-slung
Chevy and his cousin Dale riding shotgun,
big and soft and worthless except
he was three years older
and would buy the beer
if we gave him a six-pack.

Full parking lot, already littered
with beer cans and vodka bottles,
which Dale kicked through to get in line,
a case of Schlitz on his shoulder
and our money in his hand.
He must have kept the change but
he brought us a souvenir church-key
which we tried out right away.

Highway Patrol everywhere but that time
they let us off with a warning
about open containers. Then a half-hour
of madness driving north, speeders
in and out, sirens and flashing lights
where someone's new Thunderbird
went upside down in the ditch.

By the city limits the beer
was almost gone and we could cruise
the Hi-D-Ho for an hour, yell
insults at guys with dates
before throwing up on a side street.
We thought we had a grand time.

So Monday mornings after that
there were always stories to pass around
in whispers just loud enough
for the girls to hear snatches.
Joe Mack always listened
to police radio Sunday nights
and reassured us nobody
we knew had gotten killed.

"This is KOMA, Broadcasting from Oklahoma City!"

The music came, profane and innocent,
in the time before you learned of irony
and the radio was cornucopia.
You parked up on a rise, for good reception,
watched headlights crawling on the planet's edge,
all bound for someplace famous, someplace knowing,
and opened wide the dial! So fierce it seemed—
the chiming pounding squawking screaming thunder
the sound of your desire, a ruptured secret
that flooded down the plains from Oklahoma,
boasting a hundred thousand watts behind it,
and surged through muddy pickup trucks like yours,
and the doors of secret rooms:

                                    Somewhere she waits!
In this booming tide she swims with me, we are
complicit in its crimes: we know it beat
to death Your Hit Parade, poor Snooky Lanson
made to sing Heartbreak Hotel in tie and sweater
and we relishing the cruelty of our laughter;

and it breeds black leather dangerboys, their smell
of Vaseline and gasoline and Schlitz
that can make a virgin throw away her caution;

and the preachers say the truth, there is a devil
in this hot-blood music, call him Jerry Lee,
who means to get his hands upon their daughters…

It will dance us on, beyond our reservations,
beyond our shame, until our strange new bodies
become like shared possessions, shared a hundred
or a thousand ways, there is no selfishness.
And softly then, the nights—we know the nights
that ache with promise, velvet air, perfume
and smoke, a chocolate saxophone caress,
and words too slow and simple to mistake,
love you so, please don't go…

                        But you always had to go,
before the battery's potency was lost,
before the morning, when the level world
again would claim you…

                        But you would return
to touch once more the Harlem streets at evening,
the California drag strips, tumbledown
front stoops in Mississippi, candy stores
in Newark, basements of Chicago churches
where they made the music, where you longed to share it
with one you could have known so very well,
so very well, if only you had met.

Michael Harty has lived in Kansas for several decades, but his rural Texas boyhood is a continuing influence in his poetry. He is also influenced by his long career as a practicing psychoanalyst, which brings an appreciation for the struggles and complexities of human life wherever it is unfolding. His work often has appeared in the *Texas Poetry Calendar*, as well as in other periodicals including *New Letters, The Lyric, Measure, I-70 Review, Coal City Review*, and others. Among his honors and recognitions are several Pushcart nominations as well as awards in a number of sonnet competitions—the Maria W. Faust Sonnet Contest, the Nebraska Shakespeare sonnet competition, the Howard Nemerov Sonnet Award contest—and in the New Letters Poetry Contest and the Rattle Magazine Ekphrastic Challenge. An earlier chapbook, *The Statue Game*, appeared in 2015.

www.ingramcontent.com/pod-product-compliance
Lightning Source LLC
Chambersburg PA
CBHW031356160426
42813CB00082B/274